Rain Down Can

The Shearsman Chapbook Series, 2012

Seren Adams : *Small History*
Kit Fryatt : *Rain Down Can*
Mark Goodwin : *Layers of Un*
Alan Wall : *Raven*
Michael Zand : *The Wire & other poems*

hors de série
Shira Dentz : *Leaf Weather*

Rain Down Can

Kit Fryatt

Shearsman Books

First published in the United Kingdom in 2012 by
Shearsman Books
50 Westons Hill Drive
Emersons Green
Bristol
BS16 7DF

www.shearsman.com

ISBN 978-1-84861-247-1

Copyright © Kit Fryatt, 2012

Contents

Rain Down Can

Heartbreak is a man in a coat
prayer him stooping for a Gatling gun
so I have left my slippers & come
to the holy land of Walsingham
I write Mr Breakheart it's all fake
as it was in fifteen sixteen
lipstick incense bribes & drink
& he replies ccing me in on
his pavane for the birdless firmament.

Look here it's always advent
too low sun & the running plash
of pastiche on the dumb
snow fountain 24/7
though the mains supply's cut at moonrise
& this pious ejaculation
so long waited so soon comes
pp the 32.20 blues: an evergreen
bronchial hack, a shot of Advocaat

no, eggnog. Myself am present
my self is not present in the poem
in which I imagine, no, dream
Mr Bris T. Corazón
is my father not the avuncular
genius Loki he was though unknown
those sixteen—fifteen years rather
between his original's taking a 32mm
serrated wee penknife to gorge & lights

& him revenant in a coat
the day my life began
to be troubling. Anyway that 72ll. poem
is entitled 'Rain Down Can'
& it relocates a Scots
Baronial pile to Thriplow, no, Saffron
Walden in the mid-seventies:
Mr Herzeromp is driving to meet a train;
his passenger in the Mini has lost

one arm at the shoulder, his left.
The driver, something above six one
is always unsettled by closeness to a person,
never more than now since his companion
(ex-soldier, able, facile painter) is *her* brother,
she who wished you in her bed again
& took a k/b with wounding good humour.
When the nine hundred cc engine
floods, he just has to sit & wait.

She's in the station buffet.
He recognises not her but the pigskin
case as just the stuffy thing
she'd been saving for since she started earning
& eck he made her jump starting up
like that out of nowhere of a sudden.
A transistor on the countertop
plays 'Thank Heaven…' from *Gigi*; her bun,
untouched, costs 9 new p, he remembers that

& the blooming ineradicable frost
too low sun on the windscreen
framing Frozen Mutton Farquharsons

the long drive home, but not Walsingham,
the scoutmistresses in galoshes
nor the baptismal procession
at Bradwell that brought him to his knees
praying for a BB gun
nor her saying *ye brek my hairt,*

my bony ane or *the man that will nocht*
quhen he may, sall haif nocht quhen
he wald, Mr Cassechroí. No, none
of that. Doesn't that seem
odd to you? And the day after she flew
back to Tehran
one of you stood at the window
the other leant on the doorjamb
waiting the rain, mumbling Christ if, Christ.

Ghastlymake

Your fetch is here. His eyes scuttle
his oval teeth are antic pearls.

His gait is yours and the pitch of his voice.
You fall into step passing the lychgate.

Try to touch him. Your fingers start
to skim your drum-taut skin.

We call that the walls of the world.
It's quite normal and natural

that he should be the other sex
if you once reflect on it (& own

it cannot be so for everyone.)
If you take a certain turn

of mind, the seeing him will return
you home in your own prints.

But your name is what you're called,
and when you're called he'll come

carrying, carrying, carrying you home.

Oleysa's Wine Bar

Émigrés really know how to smoke, and loiter but
it's not their fidgeting that causes the underfloor
rumble in here—I don't know what does, the fridge? a nearby
laundrette?—but I can tell because everything about you, hair
eyes, skin, is tinder pale that you are unsettled by it despite it
animated—mercy! but you let me know what it means to depend on,
correspond with? to? a person—struck, I'm still ringing—midday
heads turning into the night, breath fogs, you crouch in your coat

Up Ahead of Some

I cough a lot (run-down?) so I
get up and run to Phibsborough Bridge
and down the Royal Canal to Drumcondra
Road and back. The circuit's a handy mile,
I do three or four, I'm building up slowly
and there's enough to look at, not too much:
the Cross Guns snooker hall,
canal water, locks, graffiti, swans,
the starting-something Kavanagh-envy
Northside-cringe statue of Behan.
                    At hanging hour
pass by the released, hold-alls in their hands,
wearing belts.

I'm listening to Planxty, *Planxty* (1973),
which reminds me with its opening track
that when I was eight years of age
a retired colonel gave me a picture
book of poetry for which a pale
grave child, veteran of stories
with chapters, lately looking into
Palgrave, might sense herself a little old,
so the pleasure I took was
guilty in the illustrations
to 'The Raggle Taggle Gypsies'
(derived from Child 200, a spurious
tale of the abduction of Lady Cassilis)

                    in brocade wistful, in her sark defiant
                    dancing by the campfire
                    on feet no whit darker than the shift

four & twenty years later my coarsening palette inclines
me to take ginger hair & blackwork smocking
as the colours of my constitution.
It seems I've flown
all manner of duty, lacking
the faith I yet demanded for no return.

> she finds out what she undertook
> in harbouring Johnnie Faa
> as she brewed so will she drink

I shear off for novelty's sake
thinking I'll go as far as the Phoenix Park
oh Christy, why do you turn the good Scots laird
& his ladie
into streeling culchies, *yerra & it was there last night you'd*
and that unpalatable yammering on *only wedded lord*
tho I'll forgive most anything for the not-at-all tautology *cash
        of his money-oh*

A *jalousie* ratchets up
representing in the language of furniture friendships foregone
there's a jungle in there.
Look how the rank ranks of rank rank against us, my jo
& of patriarchy!

> —Gewürz and goosequills are nice
>   but would you sleep out in the rain for me?
> —Silly goose-girl, drunk on a beau geste
>   a titus oates
>   when he's had his you won't not for dust.
> —Can't you see I'm sick, actually sick
>   (gaining weight, prone to a host
>   of recurrent minor infections)

since that seigneurial doigt lit on my choler
—Provoking object!
—Titchy lech!
—Roaring doll a-cafflin!
—Eggling toon!
—Unnatural! Cruel! *In Denial*—
—is the last refuge of a scoundrel!

The segue doesn't even pretend to suavity

tabhair dom do lámh old goat
decrepitude'll be a while yet
help me up Infirmary Road

céad míle fáilte romhat abhaile

Why I Am Not a Performance Poet

I think I would rather be more
people would want if I were
to have sex with me I feel sure

then—I'm watching a YouTube video—I

ask
        (aloud)
what
        is the font
                of that voice?

I know the difference
between font & typeface
and that properly I should
font being just an instance
of typeface, that is pattern & design

ask
        (aloud)
what
        is the typeface
                of that voice?

But I don't, because I have grown up
with word processing, which obliterated
the distinction, because in this instance
typeface is not a pun
and anyway it sounds crappy
even though or because
typeface half-rhymes with voice.

I relisten
am silenter

The others cast easy: a tall Centennial Bell
                          Centaur Roman 16pt, loveliest of its set
                          Palatino, busy and efficient

But that one: timbre warring tone
          the inflexion wrong, falling on a rhetorical question
                    wind
                              short
          easement & rest now to thee dear man
     the font
              of the voice
                          is

a hellbox of lost inhalers & empty blister packs

a self
          as
                    registering
as a bundle of optical cable

and it rises six thousand miles away
inside a person

days go by
          I hear it sometimes in emails days go by
& on painfully-awaited visits days go by
that go on too long & end in shared relief days go by

eventually I decide I am not a performance poet
          because poetry is letterpress

and I have known several people for many years
and never heard one of them speak English.

Crude Black Strap

a by-product, with kinks

(i) dom

After the long hols
the family smell
comes back perceptible.

Milk tastes sweet
in this long-waited
spring. The fat content

changes, it gets hard to froth.
Cab Calloway on the i-dock;
when did people stop

calling them avocado
pears? ho di ho di ho
The sun discloses

perfunctory hygiene,
the greasy cushion
lifted from an auction bargain

slack rubber webbing.

(ii) to get to the second person

I was teaching *Oroonoko*, wishing I might be in the cool
    odorous air, explaining about Surinam
from stuff I'd cogged off Wikipedia at lunchtime,
trying to elicit some opinions on Aphra Behn's narrative reliability
when in my habitual pedagogical jig & reel
(what was Kevin's phrase? *convulsive gesticulation*) I stumbled,
though there was nothing there to trip me
at least that got a laugh, helped them relax
so after class I debriefed myself, unpacking
my hamper of letters, less a picnic
really than a bag-lady's compulsions
but I could find nothing to explain the hagridden pressure on
    my gorge,
scarcely unusual in one whose emotional insights are less *l'esprit*
    d'escalier than *l'esprit de* out the door into a cab & in the
    departure lounge at Charles de Gaulle waiting a transfer
    to Simón Bolívar
then I contemplated a cigarette, smoking being something I
    rarely do sober
but that would mean buying 20 & a trip to the cash machine,
    or disturbing Paula
anyway, the very thought was expectorant, & I disgorged
myself of a skein that might have been the caption to an emblem
showing the beheaded king as martyr,
a trope that troubles me, since I think all execution murder,
yet am a devout republican & constitutional puritan,
a positive Slingsby Bethel of a girl,
but which I was quick—quick for me—to recognise as the eel
of frayed black belts that serves you—you—for a closet door
    handle.

(iii) mooch

The first allusion
I knew was the unvoicing
in Mrs Robinson

but now I recognise
that Cab Calloway
is the Walrus

you are not so Sweet to me
as aince ye wer
but then, how could you be?

There's been time
for sugar & elastic
to go out the gum.

Call up that pooch
& watch the mouthpiece
pucker, bugle, gnash.

Bimbo and me lit out
for a lightshow
in this Teutonic grot.

My garter's tight
as a tourniquet
but not as this vice—quite—

my head's pinned in
wrist & ankle buckle
tongue guard, and begin.

(iv) tup *honte* / a morello / a dawn! a tale!

> He's a skimmer, a trimmer
> one hell a lot slimmer
> than his avatar.

But they share moustaches
and his—his—your argent
imperial tuft.

> He's a hector, a projector
> a rotoscoped vector
> & lord protector
> of this pothole.

And like him—you—he—
hee di hee di hee

>   dooby

something between
deft & clumsy, louche & keen—

> He's a howler, a sowljeh
> a fouler of small pale souls
> an electric jowler
> a chafer, a strafer
> the inner tube off of a
> perambulator

And like him she—me—I
will fold before authority
rather than break good company
rather sell the leathers
issued to each of the brothers
upon entry & carried, usually

than deliver
a hiding kid from fleering wither.

      The skeletons fill and drain
      the ghastcat's tits
      furcate and feed her kits—

none of it begins to explain

Robinson's smokey
               chops a dubious
hand dealt Charlie
               Minnie's methadone
roar hi di hi di hi di hi
               or this fix
I've penned myself
               in labouring up & down
to pop a *moi-même* or a dappler gong.

Charlie done got fragged Minnie

you see
      it was the only armoury
you had

      squeeby squibbly dooby dooby doo wop

(v) process

I'm the glass lawyer, not much of me, none deep
most frail just when the nap of my tongue feels rough
enough to offer a few tough words on refinement—

When your mama
give you sugar you heap a half-ounce in your cup
the jar in the press fill with nutritious pitch when your mama
give you EZCheez straight from the aerosol down your throat
the achiote drain from your lips to hers because she is
        changeling-a-ling-a-ling a galvanised besom as
        whose ain't when your mama
give you evaporated milk for a tar baby a corpse flower a fly
        paper a calico ban
you sigh with release like your cherry pop when your mama
give you umami excitotoxins & frolic acid
it's to commit Autolycus to the Sanitarium & everything go
        taylor & burton when your mama
give you café mocha it is because *ugh that isn't a mocha* and the café
is full of those people performing sinister gesticulations it's
        draining when your mama
give you grief it's (what was Kevin's cadenced sentence?
a tiny but concentrated model Pietà of compassion and salutary
        feistiness)

(vi) pendent

A rose is
but the difference
between true & tea
is taste

molasses
but the difference
your chains are really
is choice

Purgatorino

—nec minus salutaris quam festivus

for Dave Lordan

Watch it in this city
faces & fruit alike
are made of wax
the idiot ox Moloch
snorts and lowers his poll
in the temple precinct
that is a kind of molehill.

Cabinetmakers here learn about furniture
through hearsay. Fruit has
names, people not so much
though their brains have been weighed
and found to weigh
about as much as brains
between 1.2 and 1.4 kilos
each, about.

Hey kiddo, hand me down that slingshot
and we'll try to redd up a bit.

Would an apple care if it
were renamed

Assassina
        Ladra
                Putana

so as to free
              'Belle Marie'
                    'Josephine Defier'
                           'None Lilly'
or a pear

Falsario, Corrutore
                    Omicidio, Grassatore
                           Uxoricido, Stupratore
which gives us

'Docteur Nelis', 'Pratt' & 'Ellis',
              'Clemence de Lacours', 'Archduc Charles'
                           & 'Bergamotte Grise'

a bunch of heavies, one butch & one in travesty, a mot,
a tom, a poisoner & a scented babyface nonce,

not bad for starters.
Despair surely will still attend us

the cabinets are choked with mementos
enough for a platoon of San Gerolamos
we haven't touched the pitchers
& pos scratched all over with pictures
& crude mottos.
              By the waters of Po
we sat down and ordered *gelati ai frutti de bosco*
and thought of your words, *ragazzo.*

They never stop having festivals.
They never stop saluting.

I began to plot & scheme
                              as argot doubledeclutched into jargon
how one might seal with a right image
the soft wax before it harden

God, it is all so reasonable!

science   disinterest   choice
health   education   housing

                    free at the point of access

non macho   unjingo   *con safos*
right to silence   free assembly   unsurveillance
               civil   disobedience
               secular   charisma
we   can   can   can   can   cancancancan
                                cancancancancancan
                    and we didididididididididididididididididid

be   particular   systematic
pragmatic   particularly   systematically
pragmatically   kind &   decent
be serious   don't take   yourself seriously

progressive   taxation   minimum
guaranteed   domestic   income
negative   interest   economy

one law   upheld   equally
          by lions   under bridges
          by oxen   in cinemagogues
                    oh mercy
                    mercy me

Failing all
that, queue nicely & well
try not to be too much of a tool.

When the lax flux
of mud & scum settles
not as here & now
shall we see them
but more as in the life to come—
congealed & sweaty, roughly
the colour of leeches

grass tories
        stuprohypnoltists
                huckstericidal gangsters

the meaner sort
      of hash-ash
                no-alternative miss Eurotrash

and if we do not all at once
balls arse & root of us
putative descendants & unsown wombs of us
sacrificial infant victims
& rootless cosmopolitans of us
fall on their necks
our scanty makings, our feeble arms
our speechless children
our skulls & faces

will fill their gaping cabinets.

'this meat-related article is a stub'

[feedback]
This meat-related article needs [feedback]
Constructive [feedback] will improve this meat-related article
This meat-related article requires cleanup to meet community
     standards
A birch besom or stringheaded mop may replace this meat-
     related article
This meat-related article has a face of crumpled linen
A corporate veil covers the face of this meat-related article
And *that* meat-related article is wearing a meat suit and regarding
a meat-related article, at the foot of a monument, in a magazine
when a boat comes into harbour carrying a meat-related article
that had lost its rudder and drifted—what is the rudder, anyway,
     of a meat-related article?
is it his cock?—
up & down in all the seas of the earth o my meet related article
o clean & proper mother there are worse places
a meat-related article can go than into the shade.

     This meat-related article is a hunter
     and his quarry too is a meat-related article.

One of them is running
but the distance never closes

          close with it only
          and its one power

one of them is running
but the distance never opens

          that of frightening
          closes to it.

Waking

Somewhere on earth
the guest who never leaves
means *husband*
the guest who never leaves
a place still has greeting to do
the guest who never leaves
an imprint goes off after a bit
somewhere on earth.

You who have been to one of the many lands of the dead
& danced when one of the many bands of the dead
struck up the waltz 'Hesitation'
tell me what we owe
to those who taste bread off the breasts of the dead
press coin into the many eyes of the dead
or I will think you don't know
or perhaps you don't know.

Corporal on furlough
having none of this
crèpe
he gobbled devilled eggs, coleslaw
porkpie jelly, T-bone marrow.
Guests
frugging all night to bayou rock
monitors & mics wreathed in pink
immortelles,
then shrieking, self-pity, tumbles
without injury, mess to clear in the stalls
tomorrow.
We passed out, seven immovable

sleepers locked in the function room till
shame
made the sun rise.

You who have been tenant to one of the many lords of the dead
and admired when he unlocked one of the many hoards of the
    dead
as if you didn't already know
it would hold everything you never had alive:
your mother's love, education, a gruff son to stay your chides
& slaps, to pick you up and birl you about
once he was tall enough.
Or perhaps you didn't know.

He tackled and took
death by surprise
as only the singular can
took back death's guest
as mourners waked
death fled.
Afterwards he was inclined
to say you've got to hold
fast, as to embrace,
death, because of all
the changes
it puts you through.
Once only to my mind
he mentioned
gaunt death has no face
as in no face.

Hospitality is very death to women
and as hard to keep from as 'when I'
in striking up conversation. We want

to put ourselves into our welcomes
not realising that *hostess*
is a maw, a death jaw, a hungry hollow
doll that will not, once it has received
us, ever let us out again.

Guests are numerous, a nation
complete in themselves, but not everyone
thank fortune, attains the condition
of guest, of a childless adult child
gripping something itself received
as a gift, that no-one would dream
of buying for herself.
Or forecourt carnations.

> It was a grim party she came
> back to, her husband's relief sitting
> like a tinfoil blanket on her shoulders.
> In time they found death
> had not cheated or revenged itself.
> Death, being the opposite of what we are,
> only did what it could
> did only what it could
>   did what it could only
> did what only it could
>   did what it only could
> taking one of the many pipeclay
> simulacra from the fire, offering.
> She stands now hesitating in doorways, through
> windows: low knowing, wicked terror
> and harried calculation pulled over her face
> determined never to go back.

Come not down our lanes or in our meadows.
Come not down our lanes or in our meadows.
Come not down our lanes or in our meadows.
Come not down our lanes or in our meadows.
Come not down our lanes or in our meadows.
Come not down our lanes or in our meadows.
Come not down our lanes or in our meadows.
Come not down our lanes or in our meadows.